Gisely Storch do Nascimento Santos
Maria Ap C. Oliveira

Teaching Portuguese:

Gisely Storch do Nascimento Santos
Maria Ap C. Oliveira

Teaching Portuguese:

Reflections and possible strategies

ScienciaScripts

Imprint
Any brand names and product names mentioned in this book are subject to trademark, brand or patent protection and are trademarks or registered trademarks of their respective holders. The use of brand names, product names, common names, trade names, product descriptions etc. even without a particular marking in this work is in no way to be construed to mean that such names may be regarded as unrestricted in respect of trademark and brand protection legislation and could thus be used by anyone.

Cover image: www.ingimage.com

This book is a translation from the original published under ISBN 978-620-2-03012-0.

Publisher:
Sciencia Scripts
is a trademark of
Dodo Books Indian Ocean Ltd. and OmniScriptum S.R.L publishing group

120 High Road, East Finchley, London, N2 9ED, United Kingdom
Str. Armeneasca 28/1, office 1, Chisinau MD-2012, Republic of Moldova, Europe
Printed at: see last page
ISBN: 978-620-8-34243-2

ACKNOWLEDGMENTS

I thank God for guiding me at all times, especially in times of doubt and uncertainty. I would like to thank my parents and friends who have stayed by my side, giving me strength and, above all, cheering me on to victory.

DEDICATION

I dedicate this work to my children Luana and Mateus, to my partner of all hours, Ari Carlos Cardoso, for his support and encouragement in yet another achievement and for his understanding of the times I was absent.

Summary

Chapter 1	**7**
Chapter 2	**13**
Chapter 3	**20**
Chapter 4	**23**

SUMMARY

The monograph presented here is the result of bibliographical research. It was motivated by many questions about traditional grammar, its history over the twenty-three centuries of its existence, as well as its applicability in schools and especially with regard to the teaching of Portuguese. The aim of this research is not to delve into the history of traditional grammar. It is simply to report on some important moments in this history and its use today. Over the twenty-three centuries, traditional grammar has often taken on a philosophical and normative character. Like the compendiums used by schools. Nor is it the aim of this work to explore the study of the normative grammar used in our schools. It will simply present ideas about its use. This will prompt reflection on the use of language in schools.

Keywords: Traditional Grammar; School; Applicability.

INTRODUCTION

Thinking about Traditional Grammar takes us back a long way, not to say a long way. We have to think about its origins, its history and its applicability to the facts of the language. Considering that traditional grammar establishes rules that are considered the best for written language, as we can see in the works of great writers. Etymologically, traditional grammar is seen as "the art of writing", considered by John Lyons to be a "classic error" (1979:9). In other definitions, it aims to establish the rules of a language and teach them to speakers of that language. Whereas it's very pretentious of her to want to teach something to someone who already has it. When students arrive at school, they are already native speakers of their language, so to believe that it is the school's job to teach them the language is a misconception. Traditional grammar has nothing to teach this speaker, if we take the perspective of communication into account.

According to historians, traditional grammar originated in Greece with Plato, Aristotle and Diomsius of Thrace. Studies show the philosophical nature of Plato's grammar. From the Alexandrians to Priscillian, in the Middle Ages and the Renaissance. And its trajectory up to the present day.

The aim of this work is not only to give a brief account of the history of traditional grammar over the twenty-three centuries of its existence, but also to show, through bibliographical research, the most diverse ways in which it has been applied in schools. We don't intend this work to analyze what kind of grammar schools study, but to contribute to reflective studies about language teaching. In view of this, there are some questions that need to be answered. How are language lessons taught, especially Portuguese language lessons? Why do students dislike Portuguese classes so much? Are there any prospects for change in language teaching? Why do students study for around twelve years and leave school unable to interpret what they read?

This text is divided into four chapters, the first of which gives a brief historical account of traditional grammar, from Plato to the present day. The other chapters are no exception, and also report on the role of the school in relation to the applicability of grammar and language teaching. Finally, we present a proposal that could be applied to Portuguese language teaching.

Since language is a living organism, it is in a constant process of transformation and needs to be studied in a social context as well, especially when it comes to valuing the mother tongue. What is the school doing in the face of these questions? What is its real role?

This work raises some questions for teachers: What is their real role as mediators of the acquisition of skills in language teaching? How are we going to train critical and reflective citizens with the practice we have seen in our schools?

CHAPTER I

FIRST WORDS

This work is justified by the need to rethink the teaching/learning of Portuguese. Although the National Curriculum Parameters (PCNs) call for Portuguese language teaching to be based on discursive genres, combining reading, textual production and linguistic analysis, there is a mismatch in terms of classroom practice.

Proof of this mismatch can be seen in the results, which show that only 35% of the students assessed by PROVA BRASIL have learned enough to complete elementary school. The assessment measures reading proficiency, disregarding other linguistic skills such as writing and speaking.

Portuguese language teachers often think of teaching language as teaching grammar in a decontextualized way. Sometimes, students graduating from elementary school, and not infrequently even from secondary school, are unable to use oral/written language as a social activity, they can't even understand what they read, they only understand information explicit in the text, as shown by the evaluations of the Sistema de Avaliagao da Educagao Basica - SAEB (Basic Education Evaluation System), applied to the final grades of elementary school.

These results show that Portuguese language teaching has failed to fulfill its role, pointing to inefficient teaching practices that value the measurement of rules and exceptions, as well as loose and decontextualized sentences. Even reading and text production activities are instruments for reinforcing the rule.

It is hoped that the Literature course will prepare professionals who will work in schools as Portuguese language teachers for primary and secondary school students. There is a whole curriculum aimed at training these professionals, as well as the legal documents that guide the common curriculum in our country.

However, even after years of theoretical and practical preparation (we're talking about internships here), when this professional arrives in the classroom, he is faced with a very different scenario from the one he envisioned during his undergraduate studies. They are now responsible for training several classes, and they have to read, interpret, write and master the standard/cult norm. In short, there are countless demands. And how do we go about the process of teaching and learning the mother tongue? Reproduce the old traditional method of teaching grammar, disguised by rare work with texts, which are used as a pretext for the grammatical approach, thus creating a false idea that they are based on contextualized grammar (GERALDI, 1997). Or work on discursive genres and their intentions, as directed by official documents, combining reading, textual production/refraction and linguistic analysis, because:

> The text is now conceived as a unit of meaning and teaching, an integrating element of the practices of reading, linguistic analysis and textual production/refraction. Consequently, the genre, as a teaching object and axis of curricular articulation/progression, aims to provide students with a broadening of their discursive horizon, by addressing different purposes, with different socio-histories. (PERFEITO, 2013, p.829)

The vision based on linguistic analysis, inaugurated by Geraldi (1984; 1997), aims to dispel possible misunderstandings about the teaching of language and grammar, proposing a change in the existing purely grammatical practice, in search of a more meaningful teaching, while still measuring the winding road that is the teaching of mother tongue, a proposal summarized in the excerpt below:

> [...] But we also believe that, within the contradictions that are present in actual classroom practice, we can look for a space for professional action in which we can outline how to do something now, in the school we have, that brings us closer to the school we want [...].
> In this sense, the issues raised here try to escape both prescription and denunciation, seeking to build some alternative course of action, despite the dangers resulting from the complexity of the subject: mother tongue teaching. (GERALDI, 2011, p.40)

The question is not whether or not to teach grammar, but how and for what purpose. If language is an instrument of social integration, through which the individual is able to intervene in the social environment, the individual's mastery and awareness of that language should be the main objective of mother tongue teaching, as proposed by the PCNs:

> When you think and talk about language itself, you are carrying out an activity of a reflective nature, an activity of linguistic analysis. This reflection is fundamental to expanding one's ability to produce and interpret texts. It is one of the many actions that someone who is considered literate is able to perform with language. (BRASIL, 1997, p. 30)

Still on the question of whether or not to teach grammar in the classroom:

> But this is a false question: the real question is what to teach and how to teach it. If the main aim of analyzing and reflecting on language is to improve the quality of language use, teaching situations should, especially in the first cycles, focus on epilinguistic activity, on reflecting on language in situations of production and interpretation, as a way of becoming aware of and improving control over one's own linguistic production. And from there, progressively introduce the elements for a metalinguistic analysis. The natural place in the classroom for this type of practice seems to be shared reflection on real texts. (BRASIL, 1997, p. 31)

The real objectives of Portuguese language teaching in the classroom become clear, as does the place that metalinguistic teaching should take. The question then arises: how is it possible for the speaker to make a metalinguistic analysis without first understanding the language itself?

This is the question that this project aims to discuss and describe through qualitative research.

The choice of the qualitative method is justified because the object of the research involves teaching practices, which are imbued with subjective factors that cannot be measured quantitatively. However, in order for there to be science, there must be methods to ensure its legitimacy, so qualitative research allows for the observation, description, reflection, discussion and analysis of data, with the aim of gaining a scientific understanding of the process.

> But without a doubt, the qualitative researcher, who considers the participation of the subject as one of the elements of their scientific work, relies on techniques and methods that have *unique* characteristics, which emphasize their involvement and that of the person providing the information. In this sense, the semi-structured interview, the open or free interview, the open questionnaire, free observation, the clinical method and the method of content analysis are perhaps the most decisive instruments for studying the processes

> and products in which the qualitative researcher is interested (TRIVINOS, 1987, p. 138).

It is therefore important to bring up the discussion of Portuguese language teaching, not with the aim of pointing out errors and culprits, but rather to reflect on teaching and then build possible paths towards more meaningful teaching that fulfills its social role.

Thinking about Traditional Grammar takes us back a long way, not to say a long way. We have to think about its origins, its history and its applicability to the facts of language. Considering that traditional grammar establishes rules that are considered the best for written language, as we can see in the works of great writers. Etymologically, traditional grammar is seen as "the art of writing", considered by John Lyons to be a "classic error" (1979:9). In other definitions, it aims to establish the rules of a language and teach them to speakers of that language. Whereas it's very pretentious of her to want to teach something to someone who already has it. When students arrive at school, they are already native speakers of their language, so to believe that it is the school's job to teach them the language is a misconception. Traditional grammar has nothing to teach this speaker, if we take the perspective of communication into account.

According to historians, traditional grammar originated in Greece with Plato, Aristotle and Dionysius of Thrace. Studies show the philosophical nature of Plato's grammar. From the Alexandrians to Priscillian, in the Middle Ages and the Renaissance. And its trajectory up to the present day.

The aim of this work is not only to give a brief account of the history of traditional grammar over the twenty-three centuries of its existence, but also to show, through bibliographical research, the most diverse ways in which it has been applied in schools. We don't intend this work to analyze what kind of grammar schools study, but to contribute to reflective studies about language teaching. In view of this, there are some questions that need to be answered. How are language lessons taught, especially Portuguese language lessons? Why do students dislike Portuguese classes so much? Are there any prospects for change in language teaching? Why do students study for around twelve years and leave school unable to interpret what they read?

This text is divided into two chapters. The first gives a brief historical account of traditional grammar, from Plato to the present day. The second chapter is no exception and also gives an account of the role of the school in relation to the applicability of grammar and language teaching.

Since language is a living organism, it is in a constant process of transformation and needs to be studied in a social context as well, especially when it comes to valuing the mother tongue. What is the school doing in the face of these questions? What is its real role?

This work raises some questions for teachers: What is their real role as mediators of the acquisition of skills in language teaching? How are we going to form critical and reflective citizens with the practice we have seen in our schools?

CHAPTER II

2- THE ORIGIN OF TRADITIONAL GRAMMAR FROM PLATO TO ARISTOTLE

Traditional grammar originated in classical Greece with Plato and Aristotle. Since Plato's time, traditional grammar has oscillated between two poles: either syntactic functions or discourse or word class functions, with the latter predominating. Rosa Mattos e Silva (1989:15). It can be seen that, to this day, traditional grammar follows one of the lines of thought already explored by Plato: the study starts with word classes and then moves on to syntactic functions. We don't have to go very far, just leaf through any traditional grammar to see this structure. Between Plato and his master Aristotle, various questions arose about problems related to language.

Still in Plato, we can see the discourse of the Sophists, who saw another problem as an object of study. They questioned that the center of the problem was not denomination, as Plato thought, but just attribution, as (Fournier Leeman, 1979:95) states, logico-syntactic prediction, therefore. Sophistry associated the appellation with speaking the truth, that is, speech that is fulfilled by effectiveness, and this led to the development of rhetoric within sophistry. They were not considered citizens, but preached the art of speaking well. What mattered to them was the power of argumentation, so this period saw a great development in rhetoric. In this way, we can see that there was no theoretical development of syntax. In Greece, with Plato, the central issue was language, without much concern for syntax. According to the quote:

For Plato, denomination is the central issue of language; and for his master

Socrates, *speaking correctly is mastering correctly.* Starting, therefore, from unraveling the problems of denomination (the origin of theories about the linguistic sign, its naturalness/arbitrariness (physei/thesei), a problem that still occupies Linguistics today), this philosophical approach founds a lexicology-semantics and not a syntax. (SILVA, 1989, p.15)

The theory of the lexicon dates back to Plato, when he distinguished between nouns and verbs. This distinction between noun and verb paved the way for an analytical understanding of the structure of thought. SILVA (1989:16). Even with these discoveries made by Plato, grammar still took a few centuries to consolidate itself, until then it was considered Philosophical Grammar.

Aristotle played a fundamental role in the history of traditional grammar, because in addition to adding to the name (noun) and verb (verb), he collaborated with the emergence of a new class of words, the conjunctions, and determined a series of distinctions called Aristotelian categories, among many categories that are not worth highlighting, since our study is more focused on a brief report than on delving into the history of traditional grammar.

2.1 Dionisio da Tracia

It took many studies and discoveries for Traditional Grammar to be consolidated in a systematic way, only from the 2nd and 1st centuries BC with Dionysius of Thrace, a period marked by the "first broad and systematic description published in the Western world". (Lyons, 1979:12) of a language with the following denomination: The Greek of Attica or Attic Greek.

Dionysius defines grammar as the "art of writing", and this period contributed greatly to the consolidation of grammar, with the distinction of eight distinct categories: name, verb, participle, article, pronoun, preposition, adverb and conjunction. History also shows that even though Plato and Aristotle distinguished (discovered) certain categories in the language, it was in Dionysius of Thrace that the lexicological formation was established, "it does not include syntax, only phonology and morphology". (M.H. Neves, 1987:116).

In the second century A.D., Apollonius Discollus appears and elaborates the first syntax of the Greek language. According to Kristeva (1974:165), this summarizes the way in which Greek grammar was organized.

> First indistinguishable from general atomism and confused in a naturalistic cosmology; then isolated - not unambiguously - as logic, a theory of abstractions from philosophy to be constructed as grammar, that is, the normative science of a particular object; it was only by passing through these different stages that language separated itself from reality and became Greek "linguistics" (1974:165).

In the light of the above text, we can see that with the organization of grammar by Apollonius Dlscolo, there was a distinction between grammar, which had previously been only philosophical, and traditional, normative grammar, and with this separation, Greek linguistics was formed. It is important to note that the grammarians of Alexandria (3rd century BC), even without knowledge, carried out their studies which contributed greatly to the development of linguistic thinking in Rome. As Jean Dubois states: Dicionnaire de Lingulstica, p.33-(34). "The grammarians of the city of Alexandria developed studies in the 3rd century BC, a series of researches which, without being properly linguistic, contributed to establishing a certain conception of language".

Varrao (1st century BC), was one of the first disciples of

Alexandrian grammarians and contributed greatly to the systematization and applicability of Greek grammar to the Latin language with the following characteristics: The grammar proposed is that of standard Latin, later called Classical Latin, as opposed to Vulgar Latin, which was the language of the discredited classes, or lower classes of the Republic and the Roman Empire. Grammar was therefore considered to be the "art of writing and speaking correctly and of understanding poets".

Etymologically, the traditional grammar of the Latin language is divided as follows, according to Silva-(1989:19):

> De lingua latina is divided into an etymology, a morphology and a syntax, which does not reach us. In etymology, he establishes the analogical relationship between words and things. Morphology, which is at the heart of his work, presents fundamental distinctions that have lasted: between variable and invariable words, establishing secondary categories to analyze the parts of speech, such as voice and tense for the verb, and applying the system of cases from Greek to Latin. This model of grammar will endure in the grammars that follow it.

2.2 Middle Ages (5th CENTURY)

With the conquests of the Roman Empire in the West, the Latin language was imposed and so was its grammar. It is worth noting that during the Middle Ages (5th century AD) the grammar of the Latin language was established by Dinatus and Priscianus, and it was in the latter that we find the first grammar of the Latin language, which was also the first in the Western world, as Silva (1989:20) states "the concepts of perfect and imperfect sentence already involve the distinction between transitivity and (non-transitivity) of verbs". Thus, with the "discovery" of syntax, we come to the conclusion that the question of transitivity and (non-transitivity) is a subject that is still latent in the normative grammars studied today. It should be noted that not only in traditional grammars, but also in other grammars, verb transitivity is addressed and questioned.

According to Silva (1989:21), the Middle Ages were the bridge linking Greece and Rome to the modern world, and the moment when Europe opened up to other worlds. Silva also highlights the analysis of the languages that surround the Roman world: Celtic, Germanic, Slavic, etc.

> It was this innovative medieval aspect, which has not been widely highlighted, that opened the way to other linguistic realities beyond Greek and Latin. This interest in non-Latin languages led to the invention of alphabets for the translation of the Christian Holy Scriptures, as well as treatises defending the right to the existence of these languages. Even grammars of the "vulgar" non-Latin languages emerged: Icelandic grammar (7th century), Anglo-Saxon grammar (10th century), Basque grammar (10th century), Irish grammar (12th century). (ibid., 23)

2.3 Renaissance to the 20th century

With the advent of the Renaissance, but precisely in the 15th century, Latin ceased to be the main language, but continued to serve as a model for other languages. The focus was no longer on the Latin language, but on the

Romanic languages, as J. Kristeva says: "the Renaissance definitively oriented linguistic interest towards the study of modern languages".

During the Renaissance, there was a great expansion of colonization and with this came the need to Christianize the colonized population, and as a consequence the need to teach the language not only Latin, but also the "vulgar" languages.

It was during the Renaissance that great grammarians emerged. And the Latin language is consecrated. Among the grammarians of this period, the humanist stands out. J.C. Scalinger (1540). According to Silva (1989:24) "Scalinger tries to delimit the field of grammar as a science, differentiating it from logic and rhetoric and from the interpretation of literary authors, and finally constructs a normative grammar of the Latin language".

Port Royal grammar emerged with the aim of breaking with the Latin model and as a response to the model put forward by the Renaissance. It brought with it a refined scientific rigor, emphasizing that its aim was to demonstrate that the structure of language is a product of reason (Lyons 1979:17).

On the subject of Port Royal grammarians, see Silva (1989:26):

> We know that in 1966, in his book Cartesian Linguistics, N. Chomsky resurrected the grammarians of Port Royal, by uncovering the links between his rationalist proposal, in opposition to the empiricist-structuralists, and the general or philosophical or rationalist grammars of the 17th-18th centuries in Europe. It is interesting to relate the fact that Chomsky's universalist rationalism is a reaction to the inductive and taxonomical theories of Bloomfieldian mechanistic descriptivism, of American structuralism

> in the first half of the 20th century, in the same way that 17th century French rationalism is a negation of the first inductive and formalist attempt to analyze language that was outlined in 16th century Western grammar.

It's important to highlight the history of traditional grammar, which began with Plato and continues to the present day. We cannot fail to mention important facts in the history of grammar, but even with the advent of the 1789 revolution, there were no changes at the heart of grammar. See Silva (1989 p. 29-30).

> It was to be hoped that the ideological changes in France with the revolution of 1789 would modify this aim of the Enlightenment. However, the system developed in the 17th century remains, only determining an orientation that goes beyond the aristocracy, thus laying the foundations for the reflection on language that began with the clashes between Sophists and Platonists and which would only be challenged in the 20th century. In our century, the "classic error" of traditional grammar - the origin of writing and the intrinsic value of the "dialect of the great poets and prose writers" - is opposed to the precedence of the oral and the non-valorization, except for extralinguistic reasons, of one linguistic variety over another. The failed enterprise of the 16th century, that of formal description based on data, will be tried again, in opposition to the rationalist grammars that tie reflection on language to reflection on the logical process of thought.

CHAPTER III

3 - THE GRAMMARIANS OF THE PORTUGUESE LANGUAGE 16TH CENTURY

3.1 - Fernao D'Oliveira

The first Grammar of the Portuguese Language dates from the 16th century and was written by Fernao D'Oliveira. Its grammar is different from Latin grammar and stands out for its originality, unlike other grammars that followed the dictates of Latin grammar.

His first grammar was published in 1536 in Lisbon, and it is worth highlighting the importance of Fernao D'Oliveira for modern linguistics. Fernao de Oliveira's grammar is divided into Orthography, Etymology, Analogy and Concerto:

- Orthography - deals with the study of phonemes, accents and prosody;
- Etymology - the origin of words;
- Analogy - studies inflection and derivation
- Concerto - part of the syntax.

His grammar deals with aspects of origin, linguistic changes and standard language, with an emphasis on clarity. See what Fernao de Oliveira himself says:

> The first and main virtue of the language is that it is clear and that everyone can understand it and that, in order to be well understood, it must be the most accustomed among the millions of people who read it and the millions of people who understand the language are the ones who will read the most and live the longest

among the prim and proper people who are not friends of much change (SILVEIRA, 1954).

3.2 - Joao de Barros

Joao de Barros, also an important grammarian of the Portuguese language. Along with Fernao de Oliveira, his work was published in the second half of the 16th century and was one of the first to provide a grammatical description of the Portuguese language.

Joao de Barros' grammar differs from others of his time in its pedagogical and normative nature. It follows the model of Latin grammars. Unlike Fernao de Oliveira, who had different peculiarities and his own style.

Joao de Barros divides his grammar into four parts: Orthography, Prosody, Etymology and Syntax.

Joao de Barros' grammatical ideas express a very clear vision of the characteristics of the Portuguese language.

3.3 - Jeronimo Soares Barbosa

Jeronimo Soares Barbosa's Grammar, of a philosophical nature, contributed greatly to the development of modern linguistics. According to Leonor Lopes Favero, Jeronimo Soares Barbosa is very important and special, "because he proposes dialogue: he exposes his positions, but expects the interlocutor to agree", and he is a forerunner "because his author sees language as a scientist: he senses, discerns, presents positions that linguistics has been privileging today". (Favero, 1996, p.258).

Our aim is not to make an in-depth study of grammarians and their grammars. It's just a brief account of their passage through history and their great importance up to the present day. The grammarians of the 16th century left us a great legacy that allows us to traverse even greater paths than those traversed by our grammarians in the course of our history. Their thoughts were so strong and consistent that they spanned almost six centuries and yet their doctrines are still very much rooted in our traditional grammars.

CHAPTER IV

4- THE ROLE OF THE SCHOOL IN LANGUAGE TEACHING: REFLECTIONS

4.1- The role of the school

The school has been based on teaching grammatical theories, disconnected from their real purpose, which is to teach language in schools. It brings with it a history of fragmented teaching of sentences and phrases that make no sense to the student. As J. Wanderley Geraldi (1987:21) states, "Language teaching has been diverted to the teaching of grammatical theory". With this practice, she makes a big mistake, since it causes students to lose interest in the study of language.

The way grammar is being applied in many of our schools has frightened students and even some teachers. We can see that students are demotivated by the subject. Who among us teachers of mother tongue, specifically Portuguese, hasn't come across situations like: I don't like Portuguese. It's a very difficult subject. I don't like the Portuguese teacher. All of this leads to demotivation, indiscipline, truancy and many other situations of conflict within the school.

The practice of Portuguese has been carried out in a mistaken, irrelevant way, causing many situations that are considered erroneous in our pedagogical practice, to substantiate this, see what Bagno says (2002: 49)

> It is therefore a real absurdity, a pedagogical crime, a huge waste of time and effort trying to teach things that are absolutely irrelevant and of no objective practical use (unless someone can convince me of the imperative need, for anyone's normal life, to

> know the difference between "adnominal adjunct" and "nominal complement", for example).... firstly, does this difference really exist, or is it just an artificial delimitation? Secondly, even if this difference does exist, does knowing it technically really make that person's oral and written performance more efficient?)

Language, understood as an instrument of social integration, as an instrument of communication, is not restricted to mere grammatical nomenclature. The speaker uses it to communicate, to produce oral and written texts that circulate in the linguistic community, texts of various kinds, which, much more than spelling and/or agreement rules, require the speaker to master their own characteristics, their communicative function. In order to acquire these skills, we need to work in a way that is totally different from what we have seen in schools.

The way grammar is being taught in schools has lost its sense of language and is restricted to the study of normative grammar. See also Bagno:

> Reducing language teaching to merely "teaching grammar" is something that no longer (or shouldn't) have any place nowadays, especially since it is disconnected from the reductionist conception of language > norm > grammar as stable, in perfect balance, with harmony between its parts, which can be well delimited, compartmentalized and described satisfactorily with the help of the categories established by Traditional Grammar. We have known for some time that many of the classifications, concepts and definitions of Traditional Grammar are flawed, incoherent and often contradictory.

Sirio Possenti (1996) goes further when he says that the role of the school is to create favorable conditions for learning to take place. See the quote:

> Perhaps I should repeat that I unquestioningly adopt the almost self-evident principle that *the purpose of school is to teach standard Portuguese,* or perhaps more accurately, to create the conditions for it to be learned. Any other hypothesis is a political and pedagogical mistake. The thesis that students who know and use non-standard dialects should not be taught or be required to master the standard dialect is partly based on the prejudice that it would be difficult to learn the standard. This is false, both from the point of view of the ability of the speakers and the degree of complexity of a standard dialect. The reasons why a standard dialect is not learned or not used are of a different order and have to do largely with dominant social values and somewhat with debatable school strategies. (...)) the problem of teaching the standard only becomes serious when it comes to teaching the standard to people who don't usually speak it, i.e. the issue is particularly serious for students from working class backgrounds, even if there are some problems arising from the differences between speaking and writing, whatever the dialect (but I insist on the hypothesis that these are probably more textual than grammatical).

Possenti also argues that the role of schools is not to teach standard Portuguese. This is a subject that he has classified and summarized in two theses: "one is of a politico-cultural nature. The other is of a cognitive nature". I use quotes mainly from Possenti to better clarify the thesis he supports:

> The political-cultural thesis basically says that it is violence, or injustice, to impose the values of another group on one social group. (...) Given that the so-called standard language is in fact the dialect of the more privileged social groups, making its teaching compulsory for the less privileged social groups, as if it were the only valid dialect, would be cultural violence. This is because, along with linguistic forms (syntax, morphology, pronunciation, writing),

> cultural values linked to so-called cultured ways of speaking and writing would also be imposed, which would imply destroying or diminishing popular values. The mistake here, it seems to me, is not realizing that the socially disadvantaged can only gain from mastering another way of speaking and writing. As long as we accept that the same language can serve more than one ideology, more than one function, which seems obvious today. This might seem obvious, but this is where the other misconception, of a cognitive nature, begins to operate. It consists of imagining that each speaker or group of speakers can only learn and speak one dialect (or one language). To put it another way: the defense of "popular" values would assume that the people only speak popular forms, and that they are totally different from the forms used by dominant groups. What applies to linguistic forms would apply to other forms of cultural expression. The hypothesis also assumes that learning a language or dialect is a difficult task, or at least difficult for certain groups or people. However, all the evidence is to the contrary. Anyone, especially children, learns ways of speaking very quickly, whether they are other dialects or other languages, and learning another dialect is relatively easy. Therefore, none of the reasons for not teaching the standard dialect at school have any reasonable basis.

Based on the thesis that we don't teach Portuguese to foreigners but to native speakers, and that the standard language should be taught in schools, what's wrong is the way it's being applied.

4.2 - Mother tongue

To support this paragraph, I must quote an excerpt from the book Fracasso do Portugues Proposta de Solugao, by the author Eurico Back (1987 p, 87; 88), who summarizes in his text how mother tongue teaching should really be in schools.

There is a very efficient school, which has never failed a single student in its many centuries of existence. It took them in without any preparation, naked and bereft of any knowledge, and sent them out examined and approved, prepared for the battle of society. It offers us a disaggregated teaching staff, virtually illiterate and lacking in pedagogical training, not responsible for good teaching performance. However, the good success continues, without us being able to attribute it to either the teacher or the student. We can only be convinced that the excellence of this school lies in the process adopted, which complies on the one hand with all the requirements of effective communication and on the other with the principles of genetic learning. The great merit of this teaching process lies precisely in the complete fusion of the data of communication with that of genetic learning, which serves a pleasant teaching exercise, perfect assimilation of the student and the friendliest human relationship between the participants in this enterprise, raised at the same time by both groups, "teachers" and "students". This school is our home and the teachers are our parents, especially the mother. The pupils are all babies, born all over the world, without any basis for study, but not for learning.

When teaching not only mother tongue, but also other subjects, the school should apply the techniques and methods used by the family, since all knowledge is inherent to the family, in other words, it happens in society. And if applied in the classroom, success is guaranteed. This will mean that the knowledge acquired by the student before school will be valued.

When children arrive at school, they already have a great deal of experience of the language, based on their experience in society and which provides great support for life. What has the school done to give continuity to this grammar? So that this teaching is not restricted to the deposit of norms established by normative grammars.

Almost all schools have valued only one textual variety, that of the great writers, forgetting that there is not just one type of text, but a huge range of textual genres, experienced in the social context in which the student lives. This type of text is despised by the school. As Bagno (2002:55) also states.

> Traditional teaching has never taken into account the infinite variety of textual genres that exist in social life, limiting itself to addressing only the most prestigious written literary genres - the short story, the novel, sometimes the chronicle, rarely poetry - and almost completely disregarding the study of textual genres that are characteristic of oral practices, mainly because of the age-old prejudice against spoken language, traditionally considered "chaotic" and "ungrammatical".

If the school's practices were based on valuing textual diversity, in oral and written form, they wouldn't just be teaching literacy, but also broadening the concepts of literacy, valuing all types of culture.

We cannot be seen as homogeneous. We are different, culturally different, with specific characteristics. The school cannot simply ignore this wealth of knowledge and focus only on isolated and fragmented texts, without coherence with the students' experiences. In other words, out of touch with their reality.

Over the years, students have increasingly shown an aversion to language teaching, motivated by the false idea that they don't know anything about Portuguese, that they can't learn Portuguese and that the subject is too difficult.

This is false, based on the fact that we are talking about native speakers of Portuguese. The answer given by the students that they don't know Portuguese is wrong.

What has the school done to change this concept formalized by the students?

It's as if the student has no voice. They are almost entirely ignored by language teachers. When students say they don't know Portuguese, they're denouncing that something is wrong with the teacher's practice. When a student says: "I don't know anything about Portuguese". He says: "Teacher, change your lesson, because I can't understand what you're getting at. It doesn't match what I know about Portuguese.

What's even more critical is when a student fails in the very language he has mastered from an early age, the language he uses to communicate, to make himself "heard". Because he is a born speaker of that language.

What we see most in schools is children repeating the year in Portuguese. But in the theater performances that the school organizes on commemorative dates, he is a ten. His speaking is perfect. He performs texts by Shakespeare, Camoes, Guimaraes Rosas and others. This same student is applauded by the teacher who, at the end of the school year, will fail him in Portuguese because, in the teacher's view, he is terrible at grammar.

And this student says he doesn't know Portuguese.

Where is the error?

In the school that fails this student?

Or the student who doesn't learn what the school teaches?

4.3 - A proposal for teaching mother tongue

In light of the above, it is clear that the teaching strategies used so far by the majority of mother tongue teachers have not met the needs of linguistically proficient students.

In this way, there is an urgent need for a teaching proposal that meets the goal of forming a linguistically proficient citizen, capable of using language as a tool for social integration.

In this chapter, we don't aim to deal with all the problems by suggesting a magical proposal that can solve all the problems we face today when it comes to teaching mother tongue. Far from it, our proposal is to suggest pedagogical ideas, teaching strategies that have been put into practice and that have produced good results, thus providing an alternative for more meaningful Portuguese language teaching.

The following report is based on the proposal to work with textual genres through didactic sequences, in line with DOLZ and SCHNEUWLY's "Oral and written genres at school".

My first contact with the proposal to work with didactic sequences was as a result of taking part in the Portuguese Language Olympics. The teacher support material provides a sequence for each genre to be worked on, namely: poetry, for the 5th and 6th year of elementary school; memoirs, for the 7th and 8th year of elementary school; chronicles, for the 9th year of elementary school and the 1st year of secondary school; and opinion pieces, for the 2nd and 3rd years of secondary school.

The above-mentioned material proposes a series of workshops that lead teachers and students along the path to appropriating the characteristics of each textual genre; poetry, memoir, chronicle and opinion piece, as well as their importance and social function, there are also workshops that work on linguistic issues pertinent to each genre such as verb tenses, the use of simple or compound sentences, adjectivization, stylistic resources, etc.

In order to encourage work with textual genres in the classroom, over the course of a semester I worked with textual sequences with a 1st year class of the Technical Course in Agriculture Integrated to High School, at the Federal Institute of Rondonia - Colorado do Oeste *Campus*. The aim of the research project, entitled "The didactic sequence as a tool for textual production: argumentative letter genre", was to investigate the effectiveness of using didactic sequences as a tool for improving students' textual production. Textual production at school has traditionally been a rigid activity, with an overemphasis on fixed rules that don't always meet communicative needs.

According to Guedes (2003), school writing, due to the extremely normative system adopted by schools, has restricted textual productions to dissertations, almost always with pre-defined schemes, repetition of information and commonplaces that nullify authorship on the part of the students, and free texts, in which there is no commitment to textuality or to the reader. Both situations are not in line with social practice, since in everyday life we are exposed to a variety of textual genres that have their own characteristics, discursive purposes and well-defined interlocutors.

> When we interact through language, we always have objectives, goals to be achieved; there are relationships we want to establish, effects we want to cause, behaviors we want to see triggered, in other words, we want to act on the other person in a certain way, to get certain reactions from them (verbal or non-verbal). This is why we can say that the use of language is essentially argumentative: we want to steer the statements we produce towards certain conclusions (to the exclusion of others). (KOCH, 2004, p. 29)

It is therefore important to make textual production more meaningful to students by creating real situations with well-defined interlocutors. The argumentative letter belongs to the argumentative field, so it becomes a fruitful genre, as argumentation is one of the most widely used social practices. Students need to understand the cause and effect relationship that an argument has. To do this, they need to know the linguistic marks of argumentation and the linguistic operators that "allow us to indicate the argumentative orientation of statements: argumentativity" (KOCH, 2004, p. 29).

In order for these skills to be developed, the didactic sequence is an instrument that enables this development, as it is a set of activities, strategies and interventions planned stage by stage by the teacher so that the students understand the proposed content or theme (KOBASHIGAWA et al., 2008). Although it looks a lot like a lesson plan, it is much broader since it covers various teaching and learning strategies and over a sequence of several days (modules, workshops, meetings).

We chose the argumentative letter genre because it is a genre with an argumentative sequence, which encourages students to express their opinions. As a theme, we worked on the Menino Bernardes Law, better known as the Spanking Law.

After a lot of research, we came up with a didactic sequence that

The research followed the stages described below to give students the opportunity to get to know the genre, create a real communicative situation and work on linguistic content appropriate to argumentation:

Goals	**Activities**	**Expected results**
Developing sequences didactics for work	1. Research the working with	At the end of the research stage it will be possible to

in the classroom with the textual genreletter argumentative.	didactic sequences in the classroom; 2. Apart from research carried out , elaborate a didactic sequence that provides the opportunity to work as generocarta argumentative.	develop a sequence didactics that meet the difficulties in working with the argumentative letter genre in the classroom.
Planning and carrying out the workshops.	Plan the workshop step by step;	It is hoped that planning makes it possible to optimize work in the classroom.
Encouraging production students' texts.	1. Criarsituagoes that favor the activity of writing; 2. Producing texts initial served as parameter to determine whether the work with didactic sequences improve textual production.	Identifying possible difficulties with generocarta argumentative.

You will work characteristics of the argumentative letter genre with students.	1. Apply didactic sequence in order to identify characteristics of the argumentative letter genre;	At this stage, the aim is that the gender characteristics are assimilated students.
Encourage the revision of texts initially.	1. Criarsituates that encourage proofreading and writing of these.	The texts are expected to be revised critically by the authors, identifying strong and weak , reorganizing the text to meet the characteristics of the genre in question.

Data analysis.	1. Compare versions (initial and final) of the texts; 2. Identify yourself there has been after working with text sequences; 3. Elaborate reports and articles.	List the advances in production quality textual work developed during the workshops. work through banners, abstracts and articles.

The sequence was divided into four modules/workshops. These are described below:

First workshop: contact with the genre and the first textual production.

In this first phase, the class was shown the aim of the project, as well as why the genre and theme to be worked on had been chosen. The students were able to answer any questions they had and then watched a documentary about the Menino Bernardo Law, where they were able to listen to experts who were both in favor of and against the enactment of the law. It was also possible to reflect on the social and cultural factors that directly influence opinions about the law. In addition to the documentary, some letters to politicians and letters from readers were made available in which the issue was addressed.

In order to work on orality, a debate was held after the screening of the documentary, at which time the students were able to express their opinions orally. At this point, we observed that the students, even without being aware of it, used various argumentative strategies: the argument from authority, refutation, construction and deconstruction of a thesis, exemplification, etc.

At the end of the first workshop, the participants produced the first version of the texts. These productions served as a strategy for identifying the students' difficulties.

Second workshop: the structure of the genre

In the second workshop, we worked on the structure of an argumentative letter. In analyzing the productions, we observed that many students have difficulty with the structure of a letter, perhaps because they are a digital generation, the letter is not a genre very present in the daily lives of our young people, however, formal communication situations require us to master this genre.

To remedy this difficulty, we worked with examples of various letters: a letter of complaint, a personal letter, a letter of introduction, an open letter and a letter to pay a bill. The students were able to identify that although each one has its own peculiarities, such as the level of language, they all have the same structure: vocative, greeting, date, farewell and signature.

Third workshop: defining positioning and argumentation.

It was possible to see that in many productions, the student's position was not clear, he presented positive and negative points, both acceptable, but he didn't take a position, it was impossible to identify what the student's opinion was.

Faced with this problem, we opted to work with the analysis of another genre, in this case, the opinion piece. We didn't focus on the structure of the genre here, because that wasn't the aim of the workshop, but rather on the arguments presented in the texts. We asked the students to read in groups and identify the position of the author of each text. This activity made it easier for the students to understand the importance of highlighting their position and thus constructing their arguments.

Fourth workshop: Final production.

At this stage, the students produced the final version of their texts, putting into practice everything they had worked on during the workshops.

Analysis of results

A comparative analysis was made between the students' initial and final productions and the evolution was clear. Many of the problems detected in the first version were remedied, and the workshop participants were able to produce more consistent arguments regarding their position on the Menino Bernardo Law.

The letters were addressed to the Chamber of Deputies, so with a defined interlocutor, it was clear to the students what level of language should be used.

Participation in the workshops was significant and they were dynamic meetings. It was clear that it is possible to work on textual production in a relaxed and meaningful way for the students.

4.4 TEACHING PRACTICES: A PEDAGOGICAL REFLECTION ON THE SOCIAL ROLE OF THE SCHOOL IN THE TEACHING OF THE PORTUGUESE LANGUAGE

The teaching of grammar in schools has been the subject of debate from different perspectives, considering that Portuguese is not only part of the academic life of students, but also of the formation of man as a critical and thinking being, capable of constructing and reconstructing knowledge.

In this sense, discussions around the teaching and learning process will always bring up a question that will guide the objectives proposed in the school environment: Why are students arriving at secondary school with so many difficulties in reading and writing and what is the social role of the school in solving this problem?

As far as the public sphere is concerned, looking for mechanisms to address this deficit in the teaching and learning process has become a necessity in an education that is constantly changing. Language is present in every society, because we interact through language and through language we seek to achieve our goals.

However, the act of reading and writing must be present in every school environment, and is a concern for all those involved in the teaching and learning process, not just the teachers who work in the area.

Possenti (1996, p.20) states that: *"Reading and writing are not extra homework tasks that can be suggested to the student as a link, but should be considered as an attitude, a necessity of life, being, however, essential to the teaching of language".*

The teaching team and the multidisciplinary pedagogical team must look for mechanisms to work on the Portuguese language in a social and cultural context, respecting the diversity and previous knowledge of the students that the school brings together, considering that the school is an environment for exchanging knowledge and the teacher is not a natural transmitter of it. Teaching is not about transmitting knowledge, but about creating possibilities through playful and dynamic lessons so that students can make their own constructions, and encouraging students to read and write constantly. Paulo Freire (2011).

In contemporary times, educational institutions are already reflecting on the need to consider social and cultural reflexes in the teaching and learning process. For quality education to take place, schools must take into account the mother tongue of our students and learn while respecting the differences that make up the richness of Brazilian society.

One aspect that must be taken into account in the problem presented is the organization of the curriculum in educational institutions, because it is organized and understood in a fragmented way, which means that we no longer understand the school as a whole, which causes individualism in the debates surrounding the teaching and learning process. As a result, it becomes common to point out the failure of the previous school, or of the Portuguese language teacher who doesn't teach the student to read and write, to interpret and to be.

In this sense, in meetings, class councils and collegiate bodies, there is always a constant concern to find a culprit for the situation, a question is always raised: How am I going to teach my subject if the student doesn't know how to read and write, interpret, how am I going to fulfill my syllabus, if I have to stop to teach grammar because the Portuguese teacher didn't teach it?
Sacristan (2011, p. 17) in his work entitled Knowledge and uncertainties about The Curriculum states that:

The concept of curriculum, from its earliest use, represents the

> expression and proposal of the organization of the sequences and fragmentations of the contents that make it up; it is a kind of order or score that articulates the episodes of the lessons, without which they would be disordered, isolated from each other or simply just put, causing fragmented learning. The curriculum performs a dual function - organizing and at the same time unifying teaching and learning, on the one hand, and on the other, creating a paradox due to the fact that it reinforces the boundaries (walls) that make up its components, such as the separation between the subjects or disciplines that make it up.

In short, these walls are very much present in discussions about teaching. The school needs to organize its curriculum, but the institution needs to be seen as a whole. Students' difficulties in Portuguese are a reflection of a deficit in education, which needs to be overcome through a broad debate.

As Petronilo puts it in 2007:

> Children are not born with school difficulties, but they appear throughout the learning process, and difficulties in reading and writing have been recognized as one of the factors that interfere with learning and the student's self-esteem. Thus, the attitude adopted by teachers in the classroom can play a decisive role in overcoming this difficulty. The teacher should convey confidence and understanding to the child and avoid transmitting distress and agony in the face of the student's difficulties.

In this sense, it is very important that teachers give students peace of mind and confidence, believing that every student is capable of learning and producing knowledge, and that they look for appropriate methods to guide the content and facilitate understanding and learning.

However, it must be considered that we need to reflect on the practice in educational institutions, there is a need for the school to teach the cultured modality of the language, but the big question is How? Grammar rules need to be seen as an instrument for reflecting on language and also on other norms.

The relationship of determination between society, culture, the curriculum and practice explains why today the curriculum is stimulated at times of change in educational systems, moments of crisis, periods of reform, innovation projects stimulate discussions about the possible rationalization schemes that can guide educational proposals. Thus, "*the curriculum should be seen as the intersection of different practices that becomes a configurator, in turn, of everything that we can determine as pedagogical practices in classrooms and schools*". Sacristan (2000, p. 26).

Schools need to learn how to teach students to read and write. Our students need to understand that in order to learn they need to have a routine of reading and writing, of interpreting, of questioning, of having reading as a possibility of dialoguing with the world, of having contact with other cultures and the knowledge necessary for human formation. This dynamic should be the goal of the institution as a whole and not just the responsibility of the teacher who works with Portuguese.

It can be seen that learning difficulties in reading and writing can be overcome throughout the educational process, with a well-organized curriculum, where the teaching team works together to overcome students' difficulties, with well-qualified teachers who are interested in overcoming these difficulties.

It is worth considering that students with this difficulty have other abilities and facilities for learning, which allows for a mutual exchange in the formation of knowledge that leads to compensating for and overcoming the difficulties presented.

FINAL CONSIDERATIONS

Faced with so many questions about the teaching of grammar and how it has been taught in schools, but especially in Brazilian schools. Everything we've witnessed is in line with the need to establish changes in pedagogical practice. In other words, in the teaching of grammar.

We have to take into account the historical process of grammar, how it became institutionalized. The way it was implemented in schools. We can see a great deal of resistance on the part of many teachers, as well as other parts of the school, to breaking paradigms, to looking for something new, which in the children's discourse is more than evident of the failure of Portuguese teaching in schools.

We continue with decontextualized, fragmented practices, armed with watertight theories, disconnected from the reality in which we are inserted and from what real language teaching should be.

In some schools, the teaching of traditional grammar is still very much present, still from the time of Plato, driven by ideologies that have nothing to do with today's reality.

It is also important to stress that the teaching of grammar cannot be disconnected from a contextualized study. It is necessary to value the mother tongue, to prioritize reading classes, with diversified texts, books, magazines and newspapers. There needs to be room for the exploration of orality, which is so latent in our children and so neglected by the school. Only then will lessons have meaning for everyone.

The role of the teacher faced with so many challenges must be creative, motivating and an interactive mediator. Opening up space for dialogue between students and teachers. They must also create bonds of affection between all those involved in the process.

Breaking the paradigm is essential, almost vital for the success of grammar teaching in schools. The changes will have to be significant in the teaching of language - in the teaching of the cultured norm, the standard norm. Not in the form established in most schools, but geared towards social practices, valuing colloquial language.

We can already glimpse very important changes in some Brazilian schools. We have seen many teachers working in a differentiated way, valuing the students' previous knowledge, what they already know about the language of their culture and bringing to their praxis the most important thing that this student has, which is their value as an important subject in the process of acquiring the standard norm established by the school. But in a different way.

There is still a lot of resistance in schools. There is a lot of confusion when it comes to preparing differentiated lessons. Many teachers are still unable to work in an interdisciplinary way, don't know how to develop projects to improve their practice and sneak out when someone wants to help them.

This attitude still exists in many schools. But not for long. Everything is moving so fast. We have many other sources of information that are moving at a rapid pace and this type of teacher won't be able to resist.

In the light of all that has been studied and exposed, our schools are still in their infancy in terms of what the real role of the school should be in terms of language teaching.

BIBLIOGRAPHICAL REFERENCES

BACK, Eurico. Failure in the teaching of Portuguese: a proposal for a solution. Petropolis: Vozes, 1987.

BAGNO, Marcos; GILLES, Gagne; STUBBS, Michael. Mother tongue: literacy, variation and teaching. Sao Paulo: Parabola, 2002.
A lingua de Eulalia: novela sociolinguistica. 11 ed. Sao Paulo: Contexto, 2001.

BRAZIL. Ministry of Education and Sports. *National Curriculum Parameters.* 1st and 2nd cycles of primary education. Brasilia, SEF, 1997.

CASTILHO, Ataliba Teixeira de. A lingua falada no ensino do portugues. 3[a] ed. Sao Paulo: Contexto, 2000.

DUBOIS, Jean. Dictionary of linguistics and grammar. Sao Paulo: Cultrix.

ELIAS, Vanda Maria (org.). *Teaching Portuguese language:* orality, writing and reading. 1st edition, 2nd reprint. - Sao Paulo: Contexto, 2014.

FAVERO, LEONOR LOPES. As concepgoes linguisticas do sec. XVIII: a gramatica portuguesa, Campinas, Sao Paulo, Editora da UNICAMP, 1996.

FREIRE, Paulo. **Pedagogy of Autonomy: Knowledge Necessary for Educational Practice**; Sao Paulo: Paz e Terra. 2011.

GERALDI, Joao Wanderlei. *Text in the classroom*: reading & production. 7aed. Cascavel: ASSOESTE, 1984.

GUEDES, Paulo Coimbra. Da redagao escolar ao texto: um manual de redagao. 2. Ed. Porto Alegre: Editora da UFRGS, 2003.

ILARI, Rodolfo. Linguistics and the teaching of Portuguese. Sao Paulo: Martins Fontes, 1993.

KOBASHIGAWA, A.H.; ATHAYDE, B.A.C.; MATOS, K.F. de OLIVEIRA; CAMELO, MH.; FALCONI, S. Estagao ciencia: training educators to teach science in the early grades of elementary school. In: IV Seminario Nacional ABC na Educagao Cientifica. Sao Paulo, 2008. p. 212-217. Available at:<http://www.cienciamao.usp.br/dados/smm/_estacaocienciaformacaodeeduca-doresparaoensininenciasnasseriesiniciaisdoensinofundamental.trabalho.pdf>. Accessed on: October 5, 2011.

KOCH, I. Interaction through language. Sao Paulo: Contexto, 2004.

SILVA, Rosa Virginia Matos. Grammatical translation and traditional grammar. Sao Paulo: Contexto, 1989.

PINTO, Edith Pimentel. O portugues popular escrito. Sao Paulo: Contexto, 1990.

POSSENTI, Sirio. Why (not) teach grammar at school. 7ª ed. Campinas: Mercado das Letras, 2001.

SACRISTAN, J. Gimeno. What does curriculum mean? In: **Knowledge and Uncertainties about the Curriculum**. Porto Alegre: Penso, 2013.
. **The Curriculum: A reflection on practice**. 3rd ed. Porto Alegre: Artmed, 2000.

PETRONILO, Silva, Ana Paula, **Learning Difficulties in Reading and in Writing**, available at http://www.ufrgs.br/ceme/uploads/1382039595Monografia_Ana_Paula_da_Silva_
Petrolino.pdf. BRASILA (DF), AUGUST 20, 2007. Accessed on 31/07/2017

MIX
Papier aus verantwortungsvollen Quellen
Paper from responsible sources
FSC® C105338

Printed by Books on Demand GmbH, Norderstedt / Germany